Everyday Materials

Wood

Andrew Langley

WAYLAND

First published in 2008
by Wayland

Copyright © Wayland 2008

Wayland
338 Euston Road
London NW1 3BH

Wayland Australia
Level 17/207 Kent Street
Sydney, NSW 2000

Editor: Annabel Savery
Designer: Ian Winton
Illustrator: Ian Winton
Picture researcher: Rachel Tisdale

Acknowledgements: Arada Ltd: 17. Corbis: 13 (Araldo de Luca), 14 (Annebique Bernard). EASI Images / CFW Images: 9 and 15 (Edward Parker). Getty Images: Cover (Ingrid Rasmussen / Axiom Photographic Agency), 6 (Georgette Douwma) 11 (Shelly Strazis). Istockphoto: title page and 18 (Dainis Derics), 4 and 21 (Maurice van der Velden), 5 (Nick Garrad), 7 (Tom Horyn) 8 (Terry Reimink), 12 (Kirill Zdarov), 14, 16 (Nico Smit), 20 (René Mansi). Shutterstock: Cover and spread head panel. UK Timber Frame Association: 10. World Land Trust: 19 both.

British Library Cataloguing in Publication Data
Langley, Andrew
    Wood. – (Everyday materials)
    1. Wood – Juvenile literature
    I. Title
    620.1'2

ISBN–13: 978 0 75025 316 1

Printed in China

Wayland is a division of Hachette Children's Books,
an Hachette Livre UK company.

Contents

What is wood?

Wood is a natural material.
It comes from trees.

Most wood is strong and hard. But some is light and bendy.

Wood can be cut and split. We use wood to make thousands of different things, from pencils to houses.

Eye spy

Look around your classroom. How many wooden things can you see?

Wood comes from trees, which grow in the earth. A tree starts as a small seed and grows bigger every year.

Did you know?

An oak tree takes more than 100 years to grow fully.

Each year a tree grows a new layer
of wood. This is called a growth ring.

Growth rings

The main part of a tree is called the **trunk**.
Smaller branches grow out of the trunk.
Leaves grow on the ends of the branches.

Cutting down trees

A person who cuts down trees is called a **logger**. A logger uses a saw to cut down a tree and remove the branches. The cut wood is called **timber**.

Next, a big truck carries the timber to a **sawmill**. Machines slice up the wood into blocks or long, thin boards.

Did you know?

In some countries tree trunks travel by water. The loggers tip the wood into a river and it floats down to the sawmill.

Building with wood

Most buildings have wood in them.
Wooden beams hold up the roof.
The floors, doors and window
frames are also made of wood.

Builders use wood because it is strong and easy to cut. Many other big things are built out of wood, such as boats and bridges.

What do you think?

Builders also use stone and **concrete** to make houses. Are these materials harder or softer than wood?

Carving and bending

Artists cut and shape wood with simple tools. This is called **carving**. Carved pieces of wood are called **sculptures**.

Craftworkers can bend wood into new shapes. They heat the wood with **steam**. The water in the steam makes the wood soft and bendy.

Eye spy

Find three pieces of **furniture** in your home which are made of wood.

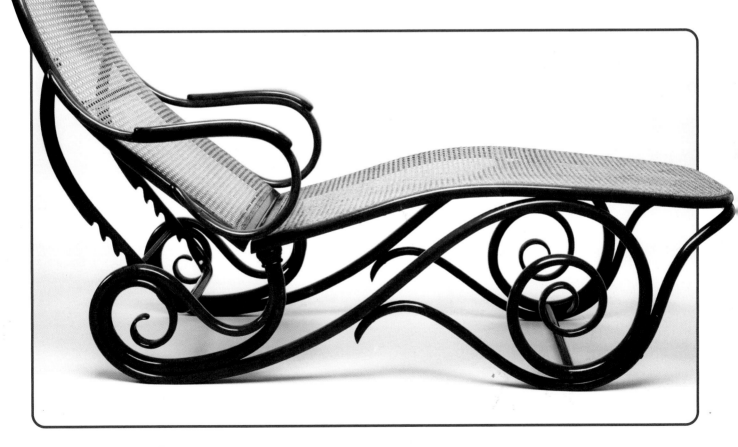

Making paper

To make paper a machine breaks the wood into tiny chips. Then the chips are boiled in hot water. This turns the wood into a soft mush called **pulp**.

Woodchips

Pulp

The pulp is spread out on a **wire mesh**. **Rollers** squeeze out all the liquid. The dried pulp becomes paper.

Eye spy

Tear a piece of paper in half. Look at the torn edge and you will see tiny hairs. These are the **fibres** that made up the wood.

Special uses

Wood is tough and springy. Cricket bats are made of wood.

Wood is also used to make many musical instruments. Pianos and guitars are made of wood.

Dry wood burns very easily. It gives out warmth. Many people heat their homes and cook food with wood fires.

Fire turns the wood into ash, which is soft and **powdery**.

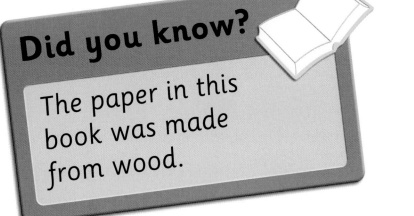

Did you know?

The paper in this book was made from wood.

Recycling

Every day people all over the world use more wood. Loggers cut down thousands of trees. Big forests are getting smaller.

We must plant new trees in place of the old ones. We will use less wood if we recycle old paper and card.

Quiz

Questions

1. What is the main part of a tree called?

2. What happens in a sawmill?

3. Why are cricket bats made of wood?

4. How can you bend a piece of wood?

5. What is paper made out of?

Answers

5. Tiny chips of wood.

4. By heating it with steam.

3. Because wood is tough and springy.

2. Machines saw tree trunks into pieces.

1. The trunk.

Wood topic web

Maths
The first type of counting machine was made of wood. It was called an abacus.

Art and design
The paper that you paint on comes from trees. The paintbrushes and pencils you use also come from trees.

History
Most toys used to be made of wood. Children had wooden yo-yos, wooden hoops and even wooden dolls.

English
Read the story of Pinocchio. It's about a little wooden puppet boy that comes to life.

Science
Trees grow when seeds are planted in the ground. First they grow a root downwards. Then they grow a shoot upwards.

Glossary

carving cutting something into a shape

chipboard board made from chips of wood

concrete hard material made from stone and water

fibre small hairs or strands which wood is made of

furniture chairs, tables and other large objects in a house

logger person who cuts down trees

powdery made of tiny, soft, pieces

pulp mushy mixture of wood fibres and water

roller heavy drum which turns and squeezes wood pulp

sawmill place where trees are sawn into pieces

sculpture piece of wood or stone carved into a shape by an artist

steam very hot mist formed when water is boiled

timber trees that have been cut down to be used for building and furniture

trunk the main part of a tree

wire mesh flat net made of crossed metal wires

Further information

Books to read

Find Out About: Find Out About Wood. Henry Pluckrose.
  Franklin Watts Ltd, 2002.

Raintree Perspectives: Using Materials: How We Use Wood. Chris Oxlade.
  Raintree Publishers, 2004.

Start-Up Science: Materials. Claire Llewellyn. Evans Brothers Ltd, 2004.

Web sites to visit

BBC Schools
http://www.bbc.co.uk/schools/scienceclips/ages/5_6/sorting_using_mate.shtml
Learn all about different types of materials and their properties.

Woodland Trust / Nature Detectives
http://www.naturedetectives.org.uk/play/
Games and quizzes by the Woodland Trust where children can learn all about trees and where they come from.

Recycling guide
http://www.recycling-guide.org.uk/wood.html
Learn all about how we can recycle wood.

Index